GUSTAVE MOREAU

Gustave Moreau

by Jean Selz

CROWN PUBLISHERS, INC. - NEW YORK

Title page: SELF-PORTRAIT, undated
Oil on canvas. Brush drawing, 16⅛″ × 13″ (41 × 33 cm)
Gustave Moreau, Museum, Paris

Translated from the French by:
ALICE SACHS

Collection published under the direction of:
MADELEINE LEDIVELEC-GLOECKNER

PHOTOGRAPHS

E. Irving Blomstrann, New Britain, Conn. – Bulloz, Paris – Clichés Musées Nationaux, Paris – Kurt Haase, Frankfurt am Main – J. Hyde, Paris – Walter Klein, Düsseldorf – Lauros-Giraudon, Paris.

Library of Congress Cataloging in Publication Data
Selz, Jean.
    Gustave Moreau.

    1. Moreau, Gustave. 1826–1898.   2. Painters–
France–Biography.
ND553.M8S4413   759.4 [B]   78-12107
ISBN 0–517–53449–5

PRINTED IN ITALY – INDUSTRIE GRAFICHE CATTANEO S.P.A., BERGAMO – © 1979 BONFINI PRESS CORPORATION, NAEFELS, SWITZERLAND
ALL RIGHTS IN THE U.S.A. ARE RESERVED BY CROWN PUBLISHERS, INC., NEW YORK, N.Y.

Two Modern Horsewomen, c. 1852. Watercolor, 6¼″ × 8¼″ (16 × 21 cm)
Former S. Higgons Collection, Paris

INTRODUCTION

The young man in houndstooth trousers and a grey derby, with gentle eyes and a well-trimmed beard, is the very image of a comfortable bourgeois in the middle of the last century. Photographed a few years later, the same man is just as elegant as ever but has a more serious air. His well-tailored frock coat is adorned with the ribbon of the Légion d'honneur, and his face is marked by a sober gravity. He might easily be taken for a mandarin of the civil service. But his name is Gustave Moreau, and one is tempted to reflect on the peculiar power of an art which, throughout the life of this stylish and dapper gentleman, succeeded in unfolding a whole procession of sphinxes, chimeras, unicorns, griffins, ghouls, harpies, winged horses and seven-headed serpents. This bestiary was indispensable if he was to perform the task to which he had dedicated himself: to be the narrator of a journey through the enchanted world of myth and legend.

If one takes a fleeting glance at the painter's work before pausing to examine it more carefully, what is striking about his choice of subjects, at a time when imaginative Romanticism was giving way to Realism, is the consistency with which he uses the same ones over and over again. In 1846, at the age of twenty, he became interested in Sappho, about whom legend and history had created a poetic and dramatic imagery which was destined to inspire the young artist. He drew in pencil, his touch already sure, *Sappho on the Edge of the Cliff*, in which there appears the lyre of Orpheus, another of Moreau's favorite subjects. Almost half a century later, about 1893 — five years before his death — he painted *Sappho Leaping from the Leucadian Cliff*. Between the drawing and this picture, approximately ten works — oils and watercolors — employed this motif, not to mention twenty-four sketches made in 1883 for costumes for Gounod's opera « Sappho » (they were in fact never used). In 1886, Sappho was on top of the cliff. In 1867, she was falling into the abyss. In 1872, the painter resuscitated her and put her back on the cliff again (see p. 24) in three watercolors which were followed by three oils depicting *The Death of Sappho*. In 1880 or thereabouts she again plunged into the sea (see p. 43), as she was to do one last time in 1893.

This is only one illustration of Moreau's persistence in adhering to the same themes in his work. Others included *Hesiod and the Muse*, drawn for the first time in 1857 and painted for the last time in 1891, after seven appearances, in black chalk, camaieu and watercolor; the *Sphinx*, the subject of a wash drawing in 1860 and of four oils and four watercolors between 1864 and 1895; and *Orpheus*, portrayed ten times, not counting drawings, between 1865 and 1891.

Gustave Moreau can thus be said never to have deviated from the road he embarked on in his early youth. This stubborn constancy is one of the most striking characteristics of his work and an outstanding feature of the man.

During the fifty-year span covered by his creative activity, painters such as Ingres, Delacroix, Corot, Courbet, Manet, Degas, all of the Impressionists and Van Gogh, Toulouse-Lautrec and Seurat, to quote only a few of the most famous names of the period — artists representing different stages in the evolution of painting in the nineteenth century — followed one another in quick succession, but Moreau must be placed outside all of the movements which were responsible for the great esthetic upheavals of the time.

Yet Moreau did not remain enslaved to those traditions so greatly respected by the painters who, like him, were devoting themselves to interpreting scenes drawn from mythology or the Bible. In his paintings he sought to express personal thoughts and to develop ideological themes. The need to invest even the smallest detail of a picture with significant symbolic or allegorical meaning led him gradually to cover his canvases with such an accumulation of significant symbols that his most understanding admirers occasionally confessed that they could not decipher them.

In order to grasp how the painter was able to fuse his intellectual vision with his particular type of pictorial expression, it is necessary to examine his work from the beginning of his career.

HOW TO BECOME AN EPIC PAINTER

In the period when Moreau decided to devote himself to painting, the Italian school of the Renaissance was traditionally regarded as the high point of the artistic education which any serious painter should undergo. But his first trip to Italy anticipated this course of instruction in a way, and even served as a prelude to his resolve to become a painter. He was not yet fifteen years old, and it was probably through the discovery of Florence and its museums that he came to discover within himself his artistic calling.

His family background was favorable to the realization of this precocious ambition. At the time of his birth, on April 6, 1826, his father, Louis Moreau, was an architect living in Paris. The following year he was appointed architect of the department of the Haute-Saône and the

Self-Portrait with Top-Hat, undated.   Pencil, 10¼" × 7⅝" (26 × 19.5 cm)
Gustave Moreau Museum, Paris

family moved to Vesoul. Dismissed four years later under Charles X for his liberal opinions, and then reinstated after the revolution of 1830, Louis Moreau became highways commissioner of the second *arrondissement* of Paris. Back in the capital again, the Moreaus (with a little daughter, Camille, born in Vesoul in 1827, who died in 1840) settled in the Rue Saint-Nicolas d'Antin, then moved to the Rue des Trois-Frères (since renamed Rue Taitbout). In 1838, Gustave enrolled as a student at the Collège Rollin.

His father, who was responsible for the preservation of several Parisian monuments and whose «Reflections on the Beaux-Arts» had been published in 1831, inevitably looked with favor on his child's penchant for drawing. A prize for drawing was the only award he received during his brief stay at the school. When, in 1841, the young man was taken to Italy by his mother, his uncle and his aunt, he received from his father a sketch-book with forty-five blank pages and was ordered to bring it back with the pages filled.

It is through these sketches — landscapes, views of cities and silhouettes of peasants — that we discover the first drawings of Gustave Moreau the artist and his first introduction to Italy and its cities — Turin, Milan, Parma, Genoa, Pisa, Lucca, Florence, Bologna, Mantua, Padua and Venice. But a serious exploration of Italian painting, which was to have a profound influence on his work, did not come until later.

Back in Paris, without neglecting his studies, he worked in a studio in the evening and soon, on the advice of Dedreux d'Orcy, another painter, began to prepare for the Beaux-Arts.

Between 1844 and 1846 (the date is uncertain), he entered the studio of François Picot. This name is known today only to very alert visitors to the Louvre who will understand why, under his aegis, Moreau could only serve an apprenticeship in the execution of the most academic and conventional sort of painting. Picot aroused attention at the Salon of 1819 with *Cupid and Psyche*, a large canvas somewhat resembling an Ingres but more akin — although more mannered and less graceful — to a work on the same subject painted by the Baron Gérard in 1798, *Psyche and Cupid*. This earned him the opportunity to decorate two ceilings of the Louvre (Room D and F of Egyptian Antiquities), on which he inflicted allegorical compositions of the utmost pomposity, *Study and Genius Reveal Ancient Egypt to Greece* (1827) and *Cybele Protects the Cities of Stabiae, Herculaneum, Pompeii and Resina from Vesuvius* (1832). We are also beholden to him for a painting hidden in the storerooms of the Louvre, *Constitutional Monarchy Defends Order and Liberty*.

It may be argued that such paintings and, generally speaking, Picot's teaching at the Ecole des Beaux-Arts (where his students included Cabanel and Bouguereau) were not likely to appeal much to Gustave Moreau. Yet perhaps it was necessary for him to fail in the competition for the «Grand Prix de Rome», in 1849, in order to comprehend that he was on the wrong track. The following year he left the Beaux-Arts.

His ambition can only be guessed at by looking at what he admired. Two painters appealed to him very strongly at the time, and his first paintings — those in which he sought to achieve what he called «epic art which would not be academic art» — were clearly influenced by them. They were Delacroix and Chassériau. Both of them were neighbors of his. The first lived on the Rue Notre-Dame de Lorette, the second on the Avenue Frochot, where Moreau himself later rented a studio. His personal relationship with Delacroix appears to have been limited to a single visit which Moreau paid him in 1850, whereas he soon developed a close friendship with Chassériau.

The romantic fire and the untrammeled technique of Delacroix and the bold harmony of Chassériau's colors and compositions were the antithesis of the cold rigidity of a François Picot and, to the young painter seeking to develop a personal style, far more stimulating. He did not resist the temptation to treat the same subjects as they, first of all those which were drawn from Shakespeare. As early as 1835, «Hamlet» had inspired Delacroix to paint *Hamlet's Farewell to Ophelia* and a number of other works over a twenty-year period. «King Lear» was painted twice by Chassériau in 1849, while «Macbeth» was portrayed in 1854 «seeing Banquo's ghost.» Moreau, for his part, painted *Hamlet, King Lear* and *Lady Macbeth*.

SELF-PORTRAIT, 1850. Oil on canvas, $16^{1}/_{8}''\times 12^{9}/_{16}''$ (41 × 32 cm). Gustave Moreau Museum, Paris

JASON AND MEDEA, 1865
Oil on canvas
80″ × 45″ (204 × 155.5 cm)
Louvre Museum, Paris

ŒDIPUS AND THE SPHINX, c. 1864
Oil on canvas
81¼″ × 41¼″ (206.4 × 104.7 cm)
The Metropolitan Museum of Art
New York
Bequest of William Harriman

11

THE POET AS A WAYFARER, undated. Oil on canvas, 70⅞″ × 57½″ (180 × 146 cm)
Gustave Moreau Museum, Paris

THE SCOTTISH HORSEMAN, c. 1854. Oil on canvas, $17^{11}/_{16}''\times14^{1}/_{2}''$ (45 × 37 cm)
Gustave Moreau Museum, Paris

Portrait of Edgar Degas
1859
Pencil, 6" × 3½"
(15.3 × 9.2 cm)
Gustave Moreau Museum
Paris

18

Hesiod and the Muse, 1858.   Black chalk, pen and brown ink, 14³/₄″ × 11³/₈″ (36 × 28 cm)
The National Gallery of Canada, Ottawa

EUROPA AND THE BULL, c. 1869. Watercolor, 6″ × 5″ (15.2 × 12.2 cm)
Wadsworth Atheneum, Hartford, Conn. The Ella Gallup Sumner and Mary Catlin Sumner Collection

Both his turn of mind and the friendship he felt caused him to be much closer to Chassériau than to Delacroix. He had been deeply impressed by Chassériau's mural for the grand staircase of the Audit Office, which was destroyed by fire in 1871. It was probably this which aroused in him a desire, which proved to be illusory and was never followed up, to emulate him and do large decorative paintings also. Chassériau's style is clearly reflected both in Moreau's drawings and in a number of his canvases, much as it can also be seen in the works of Puvis de Chavannes and, more or less accidentally, those of Degas. Yet even in works that are very similar to one another in subject and composition, Chassériau achieves a sensuality in his portrayal of evocative womanhood that Moreau, for reasons of idealism, mysticism or modesty, always refuses to express.

SOME AMBITIOUS PROJECTS

In those days an artist's whole career, his only chance to be seen by critics and by the public, his only opportunity to receive commissions and to be considered for official honors, depended on the system by which works had to be submitted to the Salon. A painter's personal style was threatened by the inevitable concern not to displease the jury, but Moreau did not dare avoid presenting works to the Salon. He exhibited for the first time at the Salon of 1852. It was then that he also made his first sale, his *Pietà* being puchased by the State for six hundred francs.

However, he cherished hopes which went beyond this and focused on vaster, more ambitious, more complex projects, both in their selection of motifs and in their execution. The immense canvas of *The Suitors* (Gustave Moreau Museum), which he began to paint in 1852 — and never completed — marked the beginning of his attempt to create monumental works, and his failure. It also reveals the genesis of his eternally unappeased desire to improve on and add to the literary themes he handled.

The size of the canvas (3.85 × 3.43 meters or 13′ × 11′4″) is such that it cannot be reproduced satisfactorily in a book. The subject is drawn from Homer. Let us recall the important though passive role played by these suitors in the «Odyssey.» Emboldened by the absence of Ulysses, which lasted for twenty years, they tried to persuade Penelope to marry one of them. But Ulysses returned and, with the help of his son, «the prudent Telemachus,» slew the suitors, who had gathered in his home in Ithaca. Perhaps it was not necessary to kill them. But Homer's epic poetry sets great store by the omnipotence of a hero who must reclaim his place by the family hearth by dint of outstanding feats of strength. It is the scene of the slaying that Moreau chose to depict. Approximately forty male figures fill the vast room, decorated with excessive ornaments and symbolic sculptures which allow the eyes no rest. Towering above the men who are slain or are about to be, the goddess Pallas Athena, who is seen as the guardian angel of Ulysses and Penelope, even though Homer refers to her as the «devastator,» appears in a luminous circle of light, like the Holy Ghost or the Blessed Virgin, raising an arm as if about to render justice. In addition, the painter, who invariably tended to expand his subjects over and beyond their original significance and who, on several occasions, was to take up his work on *The Suitors* again, introduced into the composition, in contrast to the tragic scenes, a few tranquil figures (youths holding a rose or caressing a doe) as an illustration of a poetic concept of beauty, grace and a dreamlike quality that, in its proximity to the scenes of bloodshed, made the atrocities even more moving. Thus, according to the artist, it imparted a «sublime» character to the picture. But here Moreau was replacing the cantos of the «Odyssey» with his own lyric outburst.

It was in the same year, 1852, that his father acquired from the Marquis Pazzis of Padua a town house at 14, rue de La Rochefoucauld. In 1896 it was enlarged and an additional storey added. After the death of the painter, who left it to the State, it was to become the Gustave Moreau Museum. The private apartments, the family mementoes, the painter's library and personal documents give an air of intimacy to the space surrounding the rooms in which more than eight hundred paintings and almost thirteen thousand drawings and watercolors are preserved. Some idea of the enormous project to which he devoted his life can be gained from the realization

Leda, undated
Oil, 7⁷⁄₈″ × 4¹⁄₂″
(20 × 11.5 cm)
Gustave Moreau Museum
Paris

23

SAPPHO ON THE CLIFF, 1872. Watercolor, 7¼″ × 12¼″ (18.4 × 12.4 cm)
Victoria and Albert Museum, London

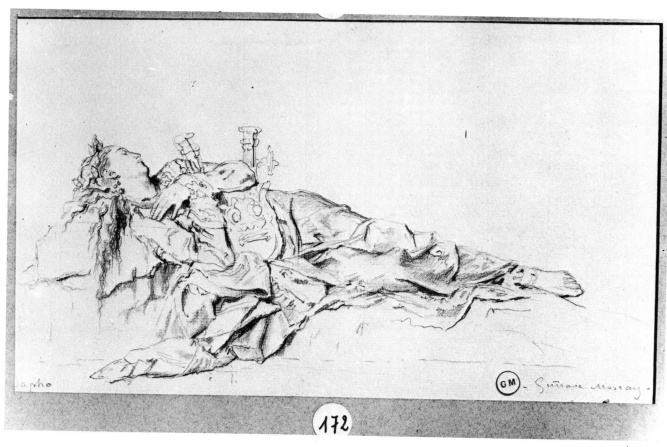

Sappho, undated. Pencil, 6¹/₄″ × 10¹¹/₁₆″ (16 × 27.2 cm). Gustave Moreau Museum, Paris

that this was only a fraction of Moreau's output, since some five hundred works are on display in other museums in France and elsewhere or are held in private collections.

Yet in the eighteen fifties, the period we are discussing, it will be seen that his work routine did not force him to deprive himself of wordly pleasures. He did not scorn the friendly little gatherings, the soirées organized by the middle-class artistic circles with which he associated and at which he was called on to exhibit his talents as a singer. (He was said to have a melodious voice.) He appears to have been an amiable and sociable man, of a happy disposition, for whom life presented no difficulties, made easy as it was because of the comfortable circumstances of his father.

BETWEEN MYTHOLOGY AND THE BIBLE

In spite of the distance he claimed to keep between himself and the artistic Establishment, Moreau remained faithful to the themes favored by the critics of his time. Their inexhaustible sources were mythology and the Bible, and it was for these themes that the national purchasing agencies expressed their preference. They bought from Moreau *The Song of Songs* for 2 000 francs and *Sulamite* for 1 800 francs, as acquisitions for the Dijon Museum. These two works were exhibited at the Salon of 1853 at the same time as a canvas on a strictly historical subject, whose descriptive title reveals the painter's preoccupations at the time, *Darius, Fleeing after the Battle of Arbela, Pauses, Spent with Fatigue, to Drink from a Pool.*

In 1855, the State purchased for the Bourg-en-Bresse Museum, *Athenians Delivered to the Minotaur in the Cretan Labyrinth* for a price of 4 000 francs. Works such as these displayed some Romantic inspiration, but this was not enough to impart an impression of tragic grandeur to the laborious study of bodies in movement. That same year he exhibited in Lyons and in Bordeaux. Approaching the age of thirty, he had already had some success with his painting. It was held in particularly high regard by a small circle of artists among his acquaintances, notably Eugène Fromentin. Yet Moreau knew that he would have to work hard before his paintings would reflect the high standards which he demanded of great art.

At the same time as he was producing pictures destined for the Salons, he started work on large compositions which he prepared carefully, using archeological documents, drawings refined by continual retracing and studies based on models, in accordance with the fundamental principles that throughout his life he would apply to his painting (ironically, those of the very school of which he disapproved).

For two years he had been painstakingly working on the vast canvas of *The Daughters of Thespius* (Gustave Moreau Museum). The daughters of King Thespius — there were fifty of them, forty being shown in the picture — were offered to Hercules by their father in gratitude for Hercules having rid the realm of a raging lion. A fine gift, worthy of such a virile hero! But the hero, seated in the midst of all of these beauties, seems lost in a gloomy study. «A cyclopean gynaeceum,» Moreau commented on the canvas. «In the center, two cippi: one supports the orb of the sun, the symbol of virile force; the other the disk of the moon, the symbol of feminine mystery. The two sexes are represented respectively by bulls' heads — powerful and tangible creatures of nature — and sphinges — a mystery both profound and elusive.» What is extraordinary, in a work in which erotic symbols abound (in the water of a basin in the foreground, for example, «irises and a lotus lift their proud and rigid stems in an erection of vegetal sensitivity»), is the fact that the assembled nudes do not radiate any eroticism. They are icy statues, which is just the way the painter intended them to be: «Animated caryatids, with the gestures, attitudes and movements of statues whose sculptural art is sober, simple and unconscious.» *The Daughters of Thespius* has been compared to the *Tepidarium* by Chassériau (Louvre), which, as it happened, was shown at the Salon of 1853. But, without any symbolism or erotic intention, the daughters of Pompeii in Chassériau's canvas seem far more likely to dissipate Hercules' melancholy than do the daughters of Thespius. Here, too, classical tradition has been cast aside by Moreau in favor of his personal concept of mythology.

In spite of the differences in their temperaments and styles, Chassériau played an important role in Moreau's esthetic evolution, and the death of this greatly admired and beloved friend in 1856 pained him very much. In tribute to the deceased artist he painted *The Young Man and Death* (Fogg Art Museum, Harvard University, Cambridge, Mass.) and dedicated it to his memory. The canvas, which was exhibited at the Salon of 1865, is not a happy example of the intrusion of literary and allegorical allusions into painting. The awkwardness of its composition is all too apparent. Between the female figure with closed eyes — Death, carrying both a sword and an hourglass — and the winged Cupid, holding a torch among the climbing plants over which flutters a blue bird, the short-legged young man seems quite embarrassed at having to hold in one hand a bunch of flowers and in the other a laurel wreath.

In 1857, another tragic event cast a pall over the life of the painter. In a letter to his friend Eugène Fromentin, he wrote, «I am undergoing a painful experience and need all my resources of moral tranquillity, but for a good many reasons they are lacking.» However, the extreme restraint which Moreau evinced in confiding in his familiar and his constant concern not to betray the innermost secrets of his life prevent us from shedding light on the causes of the crisis he was going through and which we can only guess to have been the result of a serious disappointment in love. Nevertheless we do know that he retreated into an ascetic solitude and no longer had even any desire to paint. It was at this juncture that he decided to travel to Italy, where he remained for two years, from October 1857 to September 1859.

THE ITALIAN SCHOOL

Moreau's long stay in Italy was to have several beneficial consequences. He found there the gifts bestowed by the gentle sun of an Italian October: spiritual solace and the alleviation of his sorrow. Soon after his arrival he regained a zest for work, displaying an enthusiasm attested to by his correspondence. This renewed industry was to be of major importance in his career and was reflected in the development of his technique and his esthetic perception. Moreau's true capacities and his personal style did not become apparent until later, after his return from Italy, for he needed time to digest the lesson he had learned. Without that lesson, however, he would probably not have found the road to self-discovery so quickly.

He had left Paris in the company of one of his young friends, Frédéric Charlot de Courcy, another painter. In Marseilles they embarked for Civitavecchia and reached Rome without delay. Rather than waste time strolling through the city, Moreau promptly set up his easel in the Sistine Chapel and the Borghese Palace and began to copy Michelangelo, Correggio, Raphael and the other masters whom he admired, with a determination to penetrate to the very core of their painting style by research and experimentation instead of limiting himself to a mere visual reproduction.

In the Gustave Moreau Museum, where most of his copies and preparatory drawings are preserved, one can see how conscientiously the painter applied himself to his work, which kept him in Rome until the late spring of 1858. He was especially captivated by Michelangelo.

In Florence in the last two weeks of June, Moreau continued his work as a copyist, doing either oil studies or drawings in the Uffizzi Museum, the Pitti Palace and Santa Maria Novella. Edgar Degas joined him in August, and the two men frequently worked, either together or separately, before the same paintings by Andrea del Sarto, Pontormo, Bronzino and Giovanni Bellini. Moreau was particularly attracted to Paolo Uccello, Taddeo Gaddi and, most of all, Titian. But he demonstrated this in a curious manner, by copying a copy of the *Battle of Cadore* (the original had been destroyed by fire), being probably more interested in the complicated construction of the composition than in the painting itself.

This work left Moreau little time for personal creativity. Nevertheless, in addition to some fine drawings such as *Hesiod and the Muse*, dated 1858 (see p. 20), he brought back from Rome and the Italian countryside a number of watercolors. These bore witness to the great appeal the landscape held for him and to his talents as a watercolorist, which later were to enable him to produce some of his most original work. Watercolors such as *Villa Borghese*, *View of the Colosseum*, *Villa Pamphili* (see back cover) and numerous sepia wash drawings reminiscent of Poussin recall one of the rare moments in Moreau's life when the open air and nature diverted him from his customary creative activity, which was devoted to imagining scenes that could see the light of day only within the walls of his studio.

In Venice in September he concentrated on Carpaccio. In the Scuola degli Schiavoni he copied *St George and the Dragon*, and in the Academy Museum several portions of *The Legend of St Ursula*. In December, back in Florence where Degas was waiting for him, he devoted a good part of his time to Botticelli (*Birth of Venus*), Titian (*Philip II*) and Velasquez (*Philip IV*). He also painted several watercolors. He next went to Siena and Pisa. In April 1859 he once more returned to Rome, where he does not appear to have commenced any major work except for a copy of *The Death of Germanicus* by Poussin, on display at the Barberini Palace. This copy is very close to the original, much more faithful than the one done in 1811 by Géricault, who used as a model an engraving after the original picture. (Poussin's painting, sold in 1958 by a descendant of the family of Cardinal Francesco Barberini, is today in the collection of the Minneapolis Institute of Arts.)

The Peri, 1865. Pencil heightened with sepia, white and gold, 13³|₄″ × 9¹³|₁₆″ (35.5 × 25.4 cm)
The Art Institute, Chicago

THE CHIMERA, 1867. Oil on panel, 13″ × 10¾″ (33 × 27.3 cm)
The Fogg Art Museum, Harvard University, Cambridge, Mass. Bequest of Grenville L. Winthrop

◁
PHAETON, 1878.
Watercolor, 39″ × 25½″ (99 × 65 cm)
Louvre Museum, Paris

PERSEUS AND ANDROMEDA, c. 1870
Oil on panel, 7⅞″ × 10″ (20 × 25.4 cm)
Museum and Art Gallery, Bristol, G.B.

HERCULES AND THE LERNAEAN HYDRA, 1876. Oil on canvas, 69″ × 60½″ (175 × 154 cm)
The Art Institute of Chicago. Gift of Mrs. Morton Zurcher

32

Hercules and the Hydra (Overall Study for), 1876. Pen and ink drawing, 8¼" × 5⅞" (21.1 × 15.2 cm)
Gustave Moreau Museum, Paris

Moreau's Italian wanderings finally took him to Naples, where he stayed from July to September 1859. In Rome and Florence, among the multitude of things he admired, what interested him above all in the painters of the Renaissance — much more than in the artists of the Quattrocento — was the harmonious yet skillful fashion in which they mastered the difficult composition of pictures that combined the movements of numerous human figures, and sometimes also of horses, with the geometric lines of architecture. However, he also devoted his attention to the way in which problems of color were solved in some canvases. In Naples, he made many studies in both oil and watercolor, of the frescoes of Pompeii and Herculaneum, which are preserved in the Borbonico Museum. These enabled him to rediscover themes which were dear to him and to which he was to devote the major portion of his work, themes that the painters of antiquity had drawn from mythology. These gods and heroes were the protagonists of grandiose tragedies played out between Heaven and Earth, of which Moreau saw himself as the inspired director. He felt that it was through these mythological figures that he could best reveal himself and state clearly what he wanted his art to express. For the myth, as Michel Foucault says in «Order of Things,» is truly «the locus of revelations.» Consequently it is easy to understand the great importance that Moreau attached to his study of the Neapolitan frescoes.

INTERRUPTED DREAMS

On his return from Italy Moreau seems to have made a mistake that temporarily led him into a blind alley. He was unwilling to abandon the plan that he had conceived several years before: to become a painter of monumental works. He persisted in undertaking new compositions covering some hundred square feet, refusing to take account of the fact that previous experiments of the sort (*The Suitors, The Daughters of Thespius*) had been unsuccessful, or perhaps imagining that the knowledge he had acquired of the great painters of the Italian Renaissance would now make his task easier. He was wrong. But beyond question he was a proud and stubborn man who would not allow himself to be disheartened by the difficulties facing him. He was determined to prove to himself that he was capable of achieving the goal that he had set himself. However, he did not persist in his obstinacy long enough to finish the large canvases that he had begun. In the face of so many abandoned works which account for a great part of his museum, one cannot help but wonder at the reason for this lack of perseverance.

He prepared his pictures very slowly, meticulously researched every archeological and botanical detail and traced innumerable drawings as a prelude to placing each figure in the composition. As ideas came, he interrupted the work on one canvas to begin another. Did this slow pace finally produce a weariness which caused him to lose interest in the picture he had started? Or did excessive reflection on the significance that he hoped the picture would contain — a reflection that forced him ceaselessly to change each picture and to complicate it by constantly adding new elements, and occasionally new figures — ultimately make him aware that the work he had dreamed of was impossible to create?

Perhaps all of these factors played a part in his reluctance to finish a canvas. In a creative spirit, however, each uncompleted project is an indication not so much of flagging willpower as of the counterpressure of another force, at once more muffled and more demanding, that works against the accomplishment of any task once undertaken. There are a number of examples of this phenomenon. The best known is that of Kafka, who left all of his major novels unfinished («The Castle,» «The Trial,» «America»). Throughout each of these books he was pursuing the quest for a truth which would enlighten him on the meaning of life and put an end to his continual torment. But even as he thought he was coming close to this absolute, eternal verity, it managed to elude him, and he received no answers to his questions. How, under these conditions, could he formulate a conclusive philosophy? Perhaps, for very different reasons, Moreau had a similar problem. One possible interpretation is that he hoped to depict in his large canvases a synthesis of his ideological and artistic concepts and that he put them aside when he found that he could not

Lucretia, c. 1875–1880. Wax sculpture, height 7⅞″ (20 cm). Gustave Moreau Museum, Paris

achieve this aim. Perhaps, too, he derived some sort of satisfaction from postponing until later a task the difficulties of which might well be solved some time in the future. For, as Robert Musil wrote in « The Man Without Qualities » (also an uncompleted work, as were his « Sketches for an Autobiography »), « Men are always inexpressibly happy when circumstances are such that they are incapable of fullfilling their desires. »

Moreau undoubtedly saw in his paintings much more than they were able to express. The dream he had of them was a vision more literary than pictorial. In his descriptions of his paintings he went so far as to mention elements which could not be represented graphically, such as fragrant smells and sounds. In this respect the careful notes which he wrote to explain his most important paintings are very revealing. Referring to *The Daughters of Thespius*, on which we have already commented, he wrote: « The entrance of Hercules, by night, into the chambers of the daughters of Thespius, redolent of the perfume of the women . . . » and « In the distance, fragrant gardens, the powerful scents of orange trees, lemon trees and myrtles waft intoxicatingly through the air. » On the subject of *King David* (Los Angeles County Museum of Art, The Armand Hammer Collection) he wrote: « This man on the terrace opening on to immense plains, this lamp which constantly burns against the sky, this fragrance which rises toward God . . . » And, in his comment on *Orpheus at the Tomb of Eurydyce* (Gustave Moreau Museum), we read: « Silence is everywhere, the moon appears above the small temple and the sacred walled pond. Only the drops of dew falling from the aquatic flowers make a faint and regular sound, a sound filled with gentleness and melancholy, a sound of life breaking the silence of death. »

Thus one cannot expect, and Moreau himself could not expect, colors on canvas on their own to be sufficient to depict intangible visions that his transports of poetic inspiration led him to transcribe on to paper. The leap his dream would have to take before they could be realized graphically appeared to him to be a jump over an unbridgeable gap. But it is because of these unattainable goals and ambitions, these impossible yearnings and desires, that Moreau, in his most successful works, was able to include in his paintings a host of evocative and symbolic images that, even if we cannot always decipher them, lead us in turn into a land of dreams where we wander as if in a dense enchanted forest.

In 1860, Moreau began to work on two large canvases which can be seen in his museum, both of them unfinished, *Three Kings of the East* and *Tyrtaeus Singing during Combat*. In the first painting, in which he tried to show that the three kings, who were different types, « are, in their psychological aspect, the synthesis of the soul of Humanity, » the drawing can be seen on the canvas, and the canvas itself remains visible in a number of places, while in others the color has been spread only as a sort of preparatory wash. However, the composition of the procession is striking for its graceful movement and, as always with Moreau, its moving solemnity.

The second painting, even more incomplete, depicts a confusing mass of people and horses against a rocky setting. Moreau probably knew Tyrtaeus through the Gnomic poets, who might also have directed his attention to Hesiod, and he painted the Greek poet, whose songs spurred on the Lacedaemonians in combat and led to their victory, in the company of the god Mars. « All of the young Greeks, with their beautiful heads of hair, » noted the painter, « die at his feet in the intoxication, the delirium of sacrifice. »

It is interesting to observe the prominent role assigned to the poet in the subjects chosen by Moreau. Here, in *Tyrtaeus*, we once again find the strange juxtaposition of poetry and violence that he had also used in *The Suitors*, about which he wrote: « In the midst of the purely physical scene of slaughter, to bring the mind of the spectator back to the one dream that inspires me — that is poetry . . . »

Thus we gradually begin to discern, through paintings in various stages of completion, some of the basic elements which go to make up the ideological structure of Moreau's work. The themes of the literature of antiquity, whether legendary or religious, inspired him only to the extent that he could graft his own spiritual aspirations on to them, without paying too much attention to logic if necessary. In this, mythology served his purpose better than the Bible, which nevertheless

SALOMÉ, c. 1875. Watercolor, 14⁵/₁₆″ × 9¹³/₁₆″ (37 × 25 cm). Gustave Moreau Museum, Paris

Salomé, undated
Lead pencil
23″ × 13⁹/₁₆″
(58.5 × 34.5 cm)
Gustave Moreau Museum
Paris

38

provided him with many subjects. But he did not feel completely free to take liberties with the New Testament. Curiously, he sometimes saw fit to evoke — or so he believed — a religious sentiment from a suject drawn from pagan antiquity, seeing in it, as he claimed, « a Christian quality. »

The most important and one of the least known works that he devoted to religious history was *Stations of the Cross*, which he painted in 1862 for the church of Notre-Dame in Decazeville, Aveyron. He obtained the commission through Eugène Fromentin and it was subsidized by a M. Cabrol, an industrialist. On this occasion Moreau did not waste time with lengthy preparations but painted the fourteen pictures with an unwonted celerity, being paid the sum of two thousand eight hundred francs. It is obvious that such a subject, especially if account is taken of the place for which it was intended, implicitly demands faithfulness to iconographic traditions and does not give much rein to the free imagination of the artist. Moreover, he seems to have had some misgivings about the results obtained. The work is in fact devoid of great originality, and it may well be that it was for this reason that Moreau, aware of its shortcomings, refused to sign it.

FROM ŒDIPUS TO ORPHEUS

Everything we have said so far indicates very clearly that up to the beginning of the 1860's Moreau had not yet produced a master work, a work that in the years ahead could be regarded as typical of him. It is also worthwhile underlining the importance in his career of the year 1864, when he exhibited *Œdipus and the Sphinx* at the Salon (see p. 11).

He had been interested in the subject for several years. It is to be seen, handled differently, in a pen and wash drawing dated 1860. In 1862 he was already working on squaring up a preliminary sketch of the canvas. Perhaps the limited time he devoted to his *Stations of the Cross*, the treatment of which was somewhat slipshod, can even be attributed to his extreme preoccupation with *Œdipus and the Sphinx*. As for *Œdipus*, he wrote to Eugène Fromentin on October 18, 1862, that he had vowed « not to begin until every detail, down to the smallest blade of grass, was finally decided on. »

Everything in the composition points to careful preparation and a complicated design. The painstaking manner in which colors are applied to the canvas bears witness to the meticulous, laborious care taken in its execution. That was all that was needed to impress the jury, and Moreau had his first success. The canvas was purchased by Prince Jérôme Napoléon for eight thousand francs, and on the whole critics spoke highly of it. However, a few expressed some irritation at Moreau, whom they saw as « just another Pre-Raphaelite! » And Edmond About wrote, « This Theban King is wooden ... Not a single movement, unless the wood warps, will disturb the sheets of zinc in which the artist has draped him. » But these were petulant reactions, and unimportant.

The idea of painting the Sphinx in the form of a female (the bust of a winged lioness and the face of a woman) was not new. While Egyptian sphinxes are generally animals with male human heads — although some have the head of a ram or a falcon — the Greek sphinx is feminine. However, Moreau would not have given his sphinx this particular form if he had not found a model in the picture painted in Rome by Ingres in 1808 and submitted to the Salon — *Œdipus and the Sphinx* (Louvre). The setting of rocky walls, the human fragments in the foreground and other details likewise borrowed from Ingres are proof that Moreau was not concerned about any criticism which might be leveled at him for such plagiarism, even if he was careful to change the color of the chlamys which covered Œdipus's nudity, making it green instead of red.

In several instances it will be seen that Moreau's imagination was ideological rather than plastic. He never sought to invent new forms. He found all the components of the settings, the accessories and the ornamental motifs which played such a large part in his pictures in the many documentary works in his library, in volumes on antiquity and the Orient, in « The Grammar of

Salomé (Study for), undated
Black ink on yellow paper
10½″ × 5⅝″
(26.7 × 14.4 cm)
Gustave Moreau Museum
Paris
◁

elle Tient
l'anneau
magique.

Actes de
Squelettes
d'animaux
en Naissants

▷
THE APPARITION, 1876
Watercolor
41⅜″ × 28⅜″ (105 × 72 cm)
Louvre Museum, Paris

SALOMÉ IN THE GARDEN
1878
Watercolor and gouache
28¼″ × 16⅞″
(72 × 43 cm)
Private Collection

SAPPHO LEAPING
INTO THE SEA, c. 1880
Watercolor and gouache
9″ × 5⅞″ (33 × 20 cm)
Private Collection

43

EVENING AND SORROW
c. 1882
Watercolor and gouache
$14^1/_2'' \times 7^{13}/_{16}''$
(36.7 × 19.8 cm)
The Ephrussi de Rothschild
Foundation
Saint-Jean-Cap-Ferrat, France

Ornament» by Owen Jones, in *Polychrome Ornamentation* by Racinet, a copious collection of color plates published by Firmin Didot, and even in the collection of the «Magasin Pittoresque.» It was, however, only in the interests of historical accuracy that he perused these documents; he loathed purely reconstructive painting and was not afraid of anachronisms. To put it very simply, the decorative aspect of a painting seemed to him not to need imagination.

Whatever the resemblances between the two pictures, Moreau's portrayal of Œdipus's confrontation with the Sphinx is much more interesting than that of Ingres's. The personage of Œdipus as conceived by Moreau corresponds closely, in its solemnity and spirituality, to the description he himself gave of it: «A traveler at life's most austere and mysterious hour, the man encounters the eternal enigma that assails and bruises him.» The Œdipus of Ingres, however, has the common touch of a professional model posing in a Rome studio who is playing a role for which he is not suited and is acting out an interrogation scene somewhat unconvincingly; whereas, in the case of Moreau, questions and answers have more than a superficial significance in the mute dialogue between Œdipus, with his sad and searching gaze, and the female sphinx with her seductive countenance, whose inexorable claws cling to his body. «It is an earthly chimera,» the painter described it further, «as base as matter and as attractive, that is represented by this charming woman's head, with wings suggesting the ideal but with the body of a monster, a carnivore that tears its victim to shreds and destroys it.»

It would be premature to stop here to emphasize a particular point to which we will have occasion to refer when we come to Moreau's later works: his ambivalence towards women, whom he viewed alternately as seductive and destructive. Mention might be made here of the significant presence of this ambivalence in *Œdipus and the Sphinx.*

The character of Medea, in whom Moreau become interested soon afterwards, is not of the utmost purity either. The adventures of this seductive sorceress, vindictive and murderous, with Jason are recounted in «The Argonautics,» the only known poem by Apollonius of Rhodes, revived later by Ovid, on whom Moreau drew for his painting. In his picture of 1865, *Jason and Medea* (see p. 10), he showed the couple on their return from Colchis. Jason is doubly triumphant, having conquered both the heart of Medea and the Golden Fleece. Medea, young and beautiful, still a long way removed from the terrifying woman painted by Delacroix, nevertheless lets her impassive face betray a secretive quality which cannot fail to arouse anxiety. Moreau was to take up the theme again towards the end of his life, in 1897, in a large uncompleted canvas, *The Return of the Argonauts* (see p. 83), in which he sought to expand on the meaning of the theme, summing it up in this commentary: «It is the return. It is also the fulfillment of the dream; hence a tinge of faint gravity, of serene melancholy, of sleepy intoxication, "like the diluted fragrance of orange blossoms," in all of these creatures, who are so happy and desirous of proudly filling their lungs with air, space and life.»

Exhibited at the Salon at the same time as *The Young Man and Death* (this may have been intentional: it is appropriate to recall that Death appears here with the features of a pretty young woman), *Jason and Medea* was less well received than *Œdipus.* The critics were quick to point out the extent to which it was reminiscent either of Mantegna or of Perugino. Moreau was also taken to task for the «aggressive details,» «the overabundance of trinkets,» which caused them to refer to him ironically as the «Benvenuto Cellini of painting.»

It should not be forgotten that at this period Moreau's undeniable nostalgia for the masters of the past was in contrast to the boldness and realism of artists such as Courbet, whose *Young Women on the Banks of the Seine* (1856) was by then known, or Manet, who had already painted his «scandalous» *Olympia* (1863), which as it happened was shown at the same Salon of 1865 as that at which *Jason and Medea* was hung.

However, when he did not work with a view towards acceptability at the Salon, i.e., with a concern for form that a polished painting was supposed to have, Moreau was capable of expressing himself with free and unfettered strokes that would have astounded his contemporaries if he had agreed to show them some canvases which can be seen in his museum today. One of these is *The Scottish Horseman* (see p. 13), painted about 1854, which proves to what extent his technique varied, depending on whether he was painting for himself or for others. There are several examples of this in nineteenth century painting.

However, Moreau wished to be known as a man who revived the classical tradition and it was, indeed, through the style of works such as *Œdipus* and *Jason* that he succeeded in gaining recognition. In that same year of 1865 he was invited to the Court at Compiègne. He spent a week there, for which he prepared assiduously and somewhat comically. Afterwards he repeated to his mother the «kind and friendly» words that the Emperor and the Empress had addressed to him.

It was once more Greece, the fabulous land, that provided Moreau with the subjects for two pictures that he sent to the Salon of 1866: *Diomedes Devoured by his Horses* and *Orpheus*. Scenes filled with great dramatic movement are rare among his works. He was rather the painter of a humanity which was static and might even be called silent. He himself said: «Painting is impassioned silence.» As he portrayed them, great passions were consumed by their inner fire and great sorrows appeared to be a reflection on sorrow. He preferred a man of dreams to a man of action. The violence and tragic impact of a work such as *Diomedes Devoured by his Horses* (see p. 16) may therefore be surprising, although his choice of subject can be seen to have resulted from the interest that the painter had had for a long time in the study of horses. The savagery of the scene is highlighted by the corpses recumbent on the ground of the enclosure in order to remind the beholder that Diomedes' horses fed on human flesh, but Moreau seems to be warning against excessive involvement: just as in *The Suitors* he contrasted the unexpected dreaminess of the youths with the murderous fury of Ulyses, in *Diomedes* he shows us Hercules, in the distance, perched on top of a portico, peacefully contemplating the ferocious drama that he has instigated.

In *Orpheus* (see p. 15) we have one of Moreau's most serene works. A young Thracian girl had gathered up the head of Orpheus, which, placed on his lyre, floated on the waters of the Hebrus. The details of her dress, the braids of her hair, the decoration on the lyre have been meticulously worked on by the painter who, nevertheless, has brushed in the landscape with fairly broad strokes. He was to take up the theme again, with only slight variations, in several oils and watercolors. This time the composition was not encumbered with allegorical accessories. Its special character derives from the sadness with which the girl contemplates the head of Orpheus as she holds it in her arms. However, by placing a group of shepherd-musicians in the distance, on top of a rock, with, in the foreground, two tortoises, in whom can be seen a symbol of survival in perpetuity, Moreau may have wished to express the idea that Orpheus's song could not be stilled even by his death, that he continued to live through the universal media of poetry and music.

THE CONCEPT OF FEMININITY

Gustave Moreau was now forty years old. Henceforth he was to be a well known and greatly admired painter. His *Orpheus* had made a strong impression on the public and on the critics, who were no longer sparing in their praise. The picture was purchased by the State for eight thousand francs, and the artist exhibited it again at the International Exhibition of 1867, together with *The Young Man and Death*. By this stage in his career, Moreau had not only achieved success but had also arrived at a personal style, distinguished by a classical precision in his drawing, a sober restraint in the portrayal of emotion and the choice of colors, and a romanticism in his settings, in which nature is employed to create a poetic aura. Later, he would occasionally manage to free his somewhat overly meticulous technique from the constraints that still hampered his work. But he would always remain faithful to the type of composition in which the myth-inspired imagery has a significance over and beyond the dry bones of the myth itself.

The unique quality of his painting does not reside in those effects that are strictly pictorial; rather, it is the result of his individual vision of familiar themes. An illustration of this is a work that dates from 1867 and shows a nude woman clinging to the neck of a fabulous creature, both

ST SEBASTIAN, undated
Black pencil and red chalk, 25⅝″ × 14⅜″ (65 × 36,5 cm). Gustave Moreau Museum, Paris

Fortune and the Child
1883–1886
Watercolor
Private Collection

Dureux he found the great love of his life. He did not live with her, but set her up in an apartment on the Rue Notre-Dame de Lorette, which was very near the Rue de La Rochefoucauld, where he himself continued to live with his parents. After the death of his father in 1862, he stayed with his mother. We are familiar with the features of Adélaïde-Alexandrine, thanks to several portraits he did of her, in pencil and in watercolor (see p. 92). Nevertheless there is a difference between loving a woman and loving the elements that go to make up, or supposedly make up, the fundamental characteristics of the female mentality.

Inasmuch as it is permissible to conclude that Moreau's attitude toward women can be defined by the manner in which he portrays them in his paintings, his attitude appears ambivalent. On the one hand he was capable of a tender admiration of women's beauty, to which he paid homage by creating figures bearing the names of *Eve, Aphrodite, Venus, Erigone, Europa, Dejanira* and *Galatea*; on the other hand, he was an unbending moralist who, in the spirit of the most fanatic religious traditions, saw in women the incarnation of sin and the everlasting source of evil. It was this moral viewpoint that was to express itself, with an insistence underlined by the numerous variations he made, in paintings such as *Salomé, Delilah, Messalina, The Sphinx, The Chimera*, dating from 1867, and *The Chimeras*, from 1884 (see p. 65), a huge work, never completed, which we shall return to later. He described it as follows: «This island of fantastic dreams embodies every kind of passion, fancy and capriciousness displayed by woman, woman in her essential being, a creature of instinct, obsessively drawn to the unknown and the mysterious, fascinated by evil in the form of a perverse and diabolical seductiveness.»

This may be pure rhetoric, used because it was appropriate to the subject of a particular picture. But is not the choice of such a subject significant in itself? Moreover, one of his notebooks of handwritten entries, which for the most part have not been published, contains the following observation: «The intrusion of woman into art would be an irremediable disaster. What will become of us when creatures whose mentality is as down-to-earth and practical as that of a woman, when creatures as devoid of any genuine creative gifts offer their frightful philistine opinions on artistic matters and expect that they are deserving of a hearing?» There is every reason to suppose that Adélaïde-Alexandrine never read these lines; Moreau was in fact even teaching her to paint.

THE WATERCOLORIST

In the years that followed *The Chimera* — until 1876 — Moreau's output slowed down; the quality also deteriorated. *Prometheus*, painted in 1868 and exhibited at the Salon of 1869, is a heavy-handed work, with drab colors. *Jupiter and Europa*, shown at the same Salon, likewise does not merit to be studied at length (the two paintings are in the Gustave Moreau Museum).

His work was interrupted by the war of 1870, which was a time of trial for him. He seemed uncertain as to the direction his work should take. For six years he gave up exhibiting at the Salon. In 1874 he turned down a commission to decorate the Panthéon (temporarily rechristened Church of Sainte-Geneviève, which name it would retain until 1885), as he was to refuse, six years later, to decorate the Sorbonne. He was probably aware that mural painting would divert him from the path which he had decided his art should take. It was during this period that he started to dabble in sculpture.

An entry that he made in a notebook in 1874 described plans «to model in clay and wax one or two figures that, cast in bronze, would be a better vehicle than painting for my talent and mastery in the rhythmic molding of an arabesque of lines.» However, he was under no illusions as to his chances of carrying such an enterprise through to its conclusion. It was but one item in a whole series of projects which, he said, «I am thinking about and may possibly never carry out.»

He was in fact experimenting with figurines, most of which were related to the subjects he had already handled in his paintings. They were in wax, with the exception of a rudimentary

St Michael Crushing
the Fiend or Satan
Confounded, c. 1882
Watercolor and gouache
13¾″ × 7⅞″
(35 × 20 cm)
Former S. Higgons
Collection, Paris

Salomé, molded from modeling clay on a framework of articulated wood; this seemed to be the only figure designed for studying the pose of a subject or the movement of draperies. None of them was subsequently cast in bronze. They were merely rough cast, but molded with a vigor that had nothing academic about it. He continued to be interested in this work on and off for ten years or so, after which he gave it up, leaving twelve statuettes that for a long time were unknown, being locked up and forgotten at the bottom of a cupboard the key to which was then lost. These included *Hercules, Jacob and the Angel, The Apparition, Prometheus, Autumn (Dejanira)* and *Lucretia* (see p. 35).

Moreau returned to the Salon in 1876 with three major works: *Hercules and the Lernaean Hydra* (see p. 32), *Salomé Dancing before Herod* (see front cover) and the large watercolor of *The Apparition* (see p. 41), where Salomé, one of the personages who most stimulated the painter's imagination, can also be found. He had been preparing these pictures for several years, making numerous preliminary studies.

As he confronts the hydra, Hercules is endowed with all the beauty of a solar hero, radiant in his courageous determination to destroy the monstrous serpent, the symbol of all the vices, that he has pursued and tracked down in the marshes of Lerna. Once more we discover here the setting of high vertical cliffs that Moreau frequently used to depict a truly moving and tragic landscape, notably in *The Sphinx, Orpheus, Sappho* and even *Stations of the Cross*. It is an image that must be regarded as part and parcel of the spiritual meaning that he perceived, not only in the symbolism of Christianity but in that of all religions: the sacred mountain, the holy mountain, the cosmic pillar, the path taken by man to ascend to the heavens. Moreau was later more precise about this, around 1890, in *Mystic Flowers* (see p. 82), in which, at the summit of a mountain peak, an immense lily serves as the throne of the Holy Virgin.

Salomé was the female figure who was the subject of his most extensive graphic research, the experiments in which he refined in the most minute detail the arabesques he considered so important (see pp. 38 and 48). She is also the personage who inspired some of his best watercolors. He took up this theme over and over again for several years and by 1876 had created a sequel to the famous scene of Salomé dancing: as she enters Herod's palace, light-footed but anxious, there appears before her, in a vision that is perhaps the visual embodiment of her remorse, the head of Saint John the Baptist. This is *The Apparition*. For his illustration of the sumptuous manner in which she is dressed and bejeweled and her coiffure, «piled high like a tower in the fashion of the virgins of Canaan,» Moreau made direct use of Flaubert's description of Salammbô.

It is interesting to note that it was through Moreau, the painter, that this Salomé, who was originally a literary figure, was destined to return to literature, since *Salomé Dancing before Herod* and *The Apparition* were on display in the study of the hero of J.-K. Huysmans' novel «Against Nature» (written in 1883, published in 1884). «In the work of Gustave Moreau, conceived without regard for any of the premises of the New Testament, des Esseintes finally found the realization of the Salomé, superhuman and alien, of whom he had dreamed...» «So, lost in contemplation, he examined the origins of this great artist, this mystical pagan, this visionary who could withdraw from the world long enough to be able to see, in the heart of Paris, the dazzling splendor of the cruel visions and enchanted apotheoses of past ages.»

Later Salomé was to reappear in other fine watercolors, such as *Salomé in the Garden* in 1878 (see p. 42), shown that same year at the International Exhibition, and *Herodias-Salomé* (see p. 74) in 1888.

It is almost impossible to trace accurately, year by year, Moreau's development as a painter of watercolors, for many of them are not dated. But for him they were never minor works. Like Delacroix and Chassériau, he occasionally used them as preliminary studies, but it was not long before he found in them a complete and fulfilling tool for the expression of his artistic ideas.

The medium of watercolor also enabled him to tackle subjects which he felt were especially well suited to this technique, such as small portraits, landscapes and scenes in the open air.

AN INDIAN (ARABIAN)
SINGER, 1884
Watercolor and gouac[he]
8 $^{1}/_{16}$" × 5 $^{5}/_{8}$"
(20.7 × 14.3 cm)
The Ephrussi
de Rothschild
Foundation
Saint-Jean-Cap-Ferrat
France

54

Reference has already been made to the landscapes he brought back from the Roman countryside. A watercolor dated even earlier than this — about 1852 — was *Two Modern Horsewomen* (see p. 5), which marks a break with his habitual themes drawn from mythology.

Very often the same motifs provided the subject matter for both an oil and a watercolor, or even several of them. Frequently these watercolors were for him nothing more than hasty sketches. However, it would be a mistake to regard them as this and no more. Their spontaneous quality should not blind us to the fact that they were accomplished works. It is in them that Moreau displayed his boldest technical freedom and the most remarkable facets of his personal style. «Watercolor makes a man a colorist,» said Delacroix. This is true of Moreau. And unless one were acquainted with his little paintings, such as those in which he pursued his dreams of Salomé (see p. 37) or the one he entitled *Near the Water* (see p. 72), it would be difficult to realize that his technique was capable of much greater development than the rest of his works would suggest. Only some oil sketches that he produced later, about 1890 (see p. 73), attest in the same way to those moments when he shook off all constraints in explosions of color similar to the technique later adopted by the Tachists.

However, he exhibited only those watercolors which reflected a much more detailed and elaborate treatment. Sometimes they were quite large. His *Phaeton* (see p. 30), for instance, was almost forty inches high. Odilon Redon saw it at the International Exhibition of 1875 and mentioned it in his diary «To Himself»: «Nowhere has the pictorial portrayal of the fable been executed with such fidelity. In the sparkle of its clouds, in the bold spacing of its lines, in the harshness and bite of its vivid colors, there is grandeur, emotion and a kind of fresh amazement» (May 14, 1878). In 1900, Redon did a pastel on the same theme, but his *Chariot of Apollo* (Stadelijk Museum, Amsterdam) is very different from Moreau's *Phaeton*, about which the latter commented: «It is thirty-five years since I read the superb passage from Ovid and, without my being aware of it, it has quickened my imagination and touched it with its fragrance ever since.»

Between 1879 and 1886, at the request of Antony Roux, a Marseilles collector, Moreau produced a series of sixty-four watercolors illustrating the «Fables» of La Fontaine (see p. 50). These have always been in private collections and are therefore almost unknown. Even though most of the subjects are far removed from those he had employed up until that time, he became passionately interested in this work and prepared each plate with the same care as if he were engaged in creating a gigantic composition, bringing to the task the patience and delicate touch of a Persian miniaturist. Merely to illustrate the fables involving an animal — peacock, monkey, lion or elephant — he spent more than a month making sketches in front of the cages and pits in the Paris Zoo.

Twenty-five of these watercolors were exhibited in 1881 by the «Cercle des Aquarellistes» at the Durand-Ruel Gallery, in the Rue Lafitte. The complete series was shown in 1886 at the Goupil Gallery, which was run by Théo Van Gogh. This was the only one-man show devoted to Moreau's work during his lifetime. An echo of it is to be found in J.-K. Huysmans, whom the watercolors inspired to write the following lines, in «Certains,» published in 1889: «In the room that housed them there was an *auto-da-fé* of vast skies all aflame; globes crushed by bloody suns, hemorrhages of stars flowing in purple cataracts on somersaulting clusters of clouds.» It is hardly necessary to point out that this somewhat frenzied lyricism is much more reflective of the spirit of Huysmans than it is of Moreau.

TRIALS AND HONORS

If we go back in time a little, we shall see that after the International Exhibition of 1878 (at which six of his oil paintings were shown, including *Jacob and the Angel, David, Young Moses, The Sphinx's Riddle Solved* and five watercolors), Moreau participated for the last time in a Salon, the Salon of 1880, where he exhibited *Helen on the Walls of Troy* and *Galatea* (Collection Robert

THE UNICORNS, c. 1885. Oil on canvas, 45¼″ × 35⅜″ (115 × 90 cm). Gustave Moreau Museum, Paris

THE SPHINX, 1886
Watercolor
12⅜″ × 7″ (31.5 × 17.7 cm)
Clemens Sels Museum
Neuss, Germany
◁

THE BALLAD, c. 1885
Watercolor and gouache
8⅝″ × 6⁴/₁₆″ (22 × 17 cm)
Private Collection
▷

Ballade —   Gustave Moreau

THE SIRENS, 1882
Watercolor
12⅞″ × 8⅛″
(32.7 × 20.5 cm)
The Fogg Art Museum
Harvard University
Cambridge, Mass.
Bequest of Grenville
L. Winthrop

Lebel, Paris). He was to make one more submission to the International Exhibition of 1889, but the two works he submitted were already known.

In 1884, the death of his mother plunged him into a deep state of depression. He had always seemed to be very attached to her, and it is reasonable to suppose that his desire to be near her was connected with his resolution never to marry.

It was for her, who had been deaf for several years, that he drafted little notes about each of his pictures, to give her the benefit of his comments. Today these notes are a priceless source of information on the way he saw his works. A good example is this reference to the large polyptych on wood entitled *The Life of Mankind* (see p. 67), which consisted of nine small panels and a frontispiece: «I have created, as a monumental decorative work, a set of objects representing the three phases of human existence, pictured as the three ages described in both sacred and secular mythology: the Golden Age, the Silver Age and the Iron Age. I have tried to symbolize these different ages by dividing each into compositions depicting the three phases of the day: morning, noon and night.» When the nine panels were finished in 1886, the three phases were portrayed, in the Cycle of Adam, as Prayer, Ecstasy and Sleep; in the Cycle of Orpheus, as Inspiration, Song and Tears; and in the Cycle of Cain, as Work, Repose and Death. Christ the Redeemer would appear on the frontispiece.

While devoting part of his time to the preparation of the polyptych, Moreau was also working on other paintings, notably *The Unicorns* (see p. 57), one of his most attractive works, as well as an undertaking he began in 1884: the vast picture of *The Chimeras*. He spoke of it enthusiastically in one note, one of those written for his mother, which, without undue modesty, begins with these lines: «Along with an imagination worthy of Shakespeare or Dante, I have an exquisite feeling for what is precise and logical, a characteristic of the genius of the French; this gives my work a wondrous balance and measure that appeals to the cultured, orderly and superior mind that judges me. (...) This work is dear to my heart. It is so new and pioneering that it is a graphic reproach to French art as a whole, which has never been able to raise itself to the level of a lyrical epic.»

Unfortunately, the painting was never completed. The drawing was well developed, its outlines accurately defined, but the colors did not go beyond the state of a rough sketch. Yet, taken as it is, with its fantastic setting of craggy mountains, and in the distance the city with its intricate architecture and its multitude of people, it remains one of Moreau's most curious creations. He called it a «satanic Decameron.» However, it is not Shakespeare or Dante — or even Boccaccio — that it evokes, but rather the grandiose vision of a painter who, even in his most extravagant projects, knew how to control his imagination.

By studying other unfinished works in the collection owned by the museum in the Rue de La Rochefoucauld, it is possible to see, because of the very fact that they were not completed, the care that Moreau took in the graphic construction of his pictures. *The Triumph of Alexander the Great* shows the architecture of a fabulous temple, with its towering heights and its bas-reliefs, like lace made of stone. In *Indian Women Poets*, the unusual rocky landscape is in striking contrast to the nonchalance of the female figures. The few traces of color that leave the black strokes of the drawing intact seem almost to be enough in themselves in these works, and Moreau perhaps felt that this technical ambiguity even lent them a certain charm, for he decided to sign them before they were finished.

The death of Adélaïde-Alexandrine Dureux in March 1890 was a further blow to Moreau. The instructions concerning his own burial, drawn up in 1897, in which he stipulated that he wished to have neither flowers nor wreaths, contained this moving thought for his friend: «Flowers and wreaths, on the day of my burial, should be placed on the grave of my beloved A.» It was in the state of distress in which her passing left him that he painted *Orpheus at the Tomb of Eurydice* (Gustave Moreau Museum). The workmanship was somewhat careless. He commented on the picture as follows: «The holy voice is hushed forever. The great music emanating from men and objects is dying out. (...) The soul alone remains. Silence is everywhere.»

Moreau hoped to find consolation through his work. However, no major painting can definitely be attributed to that year with the exception of a *Saint George* that he finished for the collector Louis Mante (purchased from Moreau for two thousand francs, the painting, after passing through various hands, was acquired by the National Gallery of London in 1976 for the sum of one million three hundred thousand francs. See p. 68).

It was at that time that the friendship of Henri Rupp, a former pupil, stood him in good stead. The two men had known each other for over forty years. Rupp, who had also been alone since the death of his wife, had always felt admiration and brotherly affection for Moreau. He now settled in his home and became his secretary, assistant and confidant. Moreau drew several small portraits of him in pencil and in black ink (see p. 71). It is thanks to him that the painter's writings, including the most trivial notes on loose sheets, were collected.

Although he had decided to spurn the Salons, Moreau nonetheless received recognition and honors from official sources. In 1888 he was elected to the Académie des Beaux-Arts, after having been rejected in 1882. On the subject of his election, Gustave Geffroy later wrote, in «La Vie artistique»: «The anchorite has left the cloister; the mystic has waked from the long intellectual dream that enchanted him in his cell.» In 1891 Moreau was appointed a teacher at the Ecole des Beaux-Arts, where he took over the class of his friend Elie Delaunay.

All of his former pupils — Georges Rouault, Henri Evenepoel, Jules Flandrin, Henri Matisse (whom Moreau had excused from having to take the entrance examination for the school) — testify to the high quality of his teaching. René Piot, Albert Marquet, Henri Manguin, Léon Lehman and Charles Guérin also attended his class; and outside the school Georges Desvallières was a private pupil. Even though they were still very young, their styles and attitudes differed as much from one another as they did from the paintings of their teacher. And all of them owed him a great deal.

Moreau took great care to nurture in each one of them the gifts that were uniquely theirs. The painter gave way to the teacher. He never sought to influence their views so as to make them conform to his own artistic ideas. While not evincing hostility towards new trends in art, he aimed to bolster the knowledge of the young painters by giving them a classical education. He took them regularly to the Louvre to study the old masters. It was as a result of this that Matisse, in the course of the three years he spent in Moreau's class, copied Raphael, Poussin, Ruysdael, Watteau, Chardin and Fragonard. Gaston Diehl quotes him as having said the following about Moreau: «It was an almost revolutionary attitude on his part to show us the way to the Museum in an age in which official art, dedicated as it was to the worst sort of pastiche, and living art, given over to painting in the open air, seemed to be united in trying to turn us away.»

His duties as a teacher, which he performed with so much integrity and success, did not prevent Moreau from pursuing his own artistic career. In 1891, again taking up a theme that he had treated more than thirty years earlier, he painted *Hesiod and the Muse* on wood for Count Henri Delaborde, Permanent Secretary of the Académie des Beaux-Arts (the work was acquired by the Louvre in 1961). The same year he painted *Orestes and the Furies* (Agnelli Collection, Turin) and *Arion* (see p. 75), a small canvas, very sensitively drawn, in which the Greek poet is shown, as in the legend, being saved by a dolphin in the water into which he had plunged.

A FINAL SPURT OF MYSTICISM

In 1894 Moreau commenced an ambitious work in which his visionary dreams of a universal synthesis would unfold through a kind of mythological apotheosis that soared above simple mythology. This was *Jupiter and Sémélé* (see p. 81). When he first decided to tackle the subject, he painted a rough sketch which suggested that he would limit the composition to a portrayal of the couple, akin to Ingres's *Jupiter and Thetis*, except that Moreau emphasized the gigantic stature of Jupiter. But the posture of the god, wearing the great beard with which traditional iconography had endowed him, was identical in the two pictures.

The Chimeras (Detail), 1884. Oil on canvas. Gustave Moreau, Paris

68

EVENING, 1887
Watercolor, $15^{3}/_{8}'' \times 9^{7}/_{16}''$
(39×24 cm)
Clemens Sels Museum
Neuss, Germany
▷

◁
ST GEORGE AND THE
DRAGON, 1890
Oil on canvas
$55^{3}/_{8}'' \times 38^{1}/_{4}''$
(141.5×97.1 cm)
National Gallery, London

the Argonauts, which was never completed, and sketched some preliminary drawings for *Dead Lyres.* However, he was fatally ill, and knew it; stricken with stomach cancer, he suspected his end was near. So he set about putting his drawings and papers in order and composing explanatory notes on his work lest they not always be understood. He then made his will, naming Henry Rupp his chief heir. He also committed to writing his wishes regarding his burial, which he hoped would take place without any official ceremony or eulogies. «No invitations except to my most intimate friends (...) A church service without music.»

Gustave Moreau died on April 18, 1898, at the age of seventy-two. He bequeathed his house on the Rue de La Rochefoucauld to the State, with all the works in it and instructions that these should all be made accessible to the public. Under a law passed on March 30, 1902, it was given the status of a national museum. The Gustave Moreau Museum, of which Georges Rouault was the first curator, was opened to the public at the beginning of 1903.

THE TERRITORY OF SYMBOLISM

In any attempt to understand Moreau's place in the Symbolist movement — or, rather, his place in relation to it — it is advisable to distinguish between the painters who actually called themselves Symbolists and those whom critics have since classified under this heading. In this respect, and in spite of its interest and importance, the «Symbolism in Europe» exhibition held in Rotterdam in 1976 and then later at the Grand-Palais in Paris might cause some confusion.

It must first be recognized that any movement has predecessors. We know the antecedents of Impressionism, Expressionism and Surrealism. Symbolism belongs to all periods of painting, beginning with the most primitive. In its manifestations of metaphysical and religious thought, Oriental and Byzantine art are its most obvious exponents. A study of the numerous formulas evolved by modern art suggests that they have been permeated by a conspicuous symbolism, while expressed in a new language.

The symbolism of the painters of the last fifteen years of the nineteenth century, who were responsible for a movement formed as a reaction against the anecdotal realism favored by the official Salons, was expressed in so many different ways that it might well be foolish to try to bring them together under the blanket of a single ideology. The very meaning of the word «Symbolism» is not without its ambiguities. As Albert-Marie Schmidt said, «It is constantly evading the enticing lures of criticism. It defies definition.» The definition that Jean Moréas arrived at in his «Manifesto on Symbolism» (published in the literary supplement of «Figaro» on September 18, 1886) is acceptable only because it is extremely vague: «Symbolist poetry seeks to clothe the Idea in a tangible form that, however, is not an end in itself but, even while serving to express the Idea, remains subservient to it.»

Curiously, this definition is much more applicable to painting than to poetry, for the spirit of Symbolist painting and its choice of themes separate it so clearly from Symbolist poetry that it is quite evident that the word «Symbolism» did not have the same significance for painters as for poets. Its significance was much more clear-cut to painters than to poets, whose references to Symbolists tended only too often to be incorrect. They were better advised to entrust their reputations to Baudelaire's theory of correlations, which, in an article on Moreau (in the «Gazette des Beaux-Arts) published in July 1886, Ary Renan expounded as follows: «Baudelaire called the feeling of correlation the feeling that, in poetic creations, causes us to discover a secret parallelism between each state of the soul and a corresponding state of inanimate nature.»

The dominant factor in Symbolist poets such as Mallarmé, Verlaine, Moréas, Rodenbach, Verhaeren, Gustave Kahn, Samain, Laforgue, René Ghil, Maeterlink and Viélé-Griffin was the expression of what people were pleased to call a «state of mind» much more than an esoteric collection of images which could only be deciphered if their underlying ideas were known. This state of mind was invariably one of languor, boredom, sadness, nostalgia, vague unsatisfied

Portrait of Henri Rupp, undated. Pen and ink drawing with sepia wash, 9″ × 7¹/₁₆″ (23 × 18 cm)
Gustave Moreau Museum, Paris

NEAR THE WATER, undated. Watercolor $10^{5}/_{8}'' \times 14^{9}/_{16}''$ (27 $\times$ 37 cm)
Gustave Moreau Museum, Paris

ABSTRACT SKETCH, c. 1890. Oil on panel, $8\frac{3}{8}'' \times 10\frac{5}{8}''$ (21.4 × 27 cm)
Gustave Moreau Museum, Paris

HERODIAS-SALOMÉ
1888
Watercolor and gouache
$8^{13}/_{16}'' \times 6^{1}/_{4}''$
(25.5 × 16 cm)
Private Collection

◁

▷
ARION, 1891
Oil on canvas
$17^{11}/_{16}'' \times 14^{1}/_{8}''$
(45.5 × 37 cm)
Museum
of the Petit-Palais
Paris

74

Gustave Moreau
à son bien cher confrère et ami J. Chaplain —   —1891—

THE BIRTH OF VENUS (SKETCH), undated. Oil on canvas, $15^3/_4'' \times 24^7/_{16}''$ (40 × 62 cm)
Gustave Moreau Museum, Paris

Seated Nude, undated
Brown ink, 13³⁄₄″ × 7¹³⁄₁₆″
(35.2 × 19.9 cm)
Gustave Moreau Museum
Paris

Portrait of a Woman, undated. Pencil, 10⁵/₁₆″ × 7¹¹/₁₆″ (26.2 × 19.6 cm)
Gustave Moreau Museum, Paris

Sketch of a Woman Putting on her Black Gloves, undated.   India ink, 14³/₁₆″ × 9⁷/₁₆″ (36 × 24 cm)
Gustave Moreau Museum, Paris

Sémélé, undated. Pencil on yellow paper, 16³/₄″ × 11¹¹/₁₆″ (42.5 × 29.7 cm)
Gustave Moreau Museum, Paris

JUPITER AND SÉMÉLÉ (Detail), 1894–1895. Oil on canvas. Gustave Moreau Museum, Paris

THE MYSTICAL FLOWER
c. 1890
Oil on canvas
99½" × 54"
(253 × 137 cm)
Gustave Moreau Museum
Paris

◁

▷
THE RETURN
OF THE ARGONAUTS
(Detail), 1897
Oil on canvas
Gustave Moreau Museum
Paris

MODERN WOMAN
undated
Watercolor
7 $\frac{11}{16}$" × 4 $\frac{15}{16}$"
(19.5 × 12.5 cm)
Gustave Moreau
Museum
Paris

Little Girl, undated
India ink
8 ⅝″ × 4½″ (22 × 11.5 cm)
Gustave Moreau Museum
Paris

PORTRAIT OF A WOMAN
undated
Watercolor
$9^{1}/_{16}'' \times 5^{7}/_{16}''$
(23 × 13.9 cm)
Gustave Moreau Museum
Paris
◁

▷
PAULINE MOREAU
undated
Pencil and watercolor
$14^{3}/_{16}'' \times 10^{5}/_{8}''$
(36 × 27 cm)
Gustave Moreau Museum
Paris

Portrait of the Artist's Mother with Glasses, undated. Pencil, 11⅝" × 8¼" (29.5 × 21 cm)
Gustave Moreau Museum, Paris

PORTRAIT OF MADAME X, undated. Watercolor, $6^{7}/_{8}'' \times 4^{15}/_{16}''$ (17.5 × 12.5 cm).
Gustave Moreau Museum, Paris

desires, a latent anxiety. Empty, sad Sundays, oppressive, inhuman cities, twilights of the day and of life and Verlaine's «Les sanglots longs des violons de l'automne» (Autumn begins; her violins sigh and sob) — this is the typical atmosphere of Symbolist poetry and of its imagery. In its vocabulary, in which «apathy» is a key word, shadows are «feline,» souls are «lonely,» flesh is «opalescent,» «the roses are faded and the lilies dying.»

However, a few poets were inspired by contemporary painters, notably by Moreau, to whom Stuart Merrill dedicated a sonnet and José-Maria de Hérédia a poem entitled «Jason and Medea.» In addition, some of Moreau's paintings had titles that were echoed in several articles in «L'Ombre ardente,» published by Jean Lorrain in 1897: *The Chimera, Sappho Dead, Galatea, The Sirens, The Young Man and Death.* The painter received a copy of the book with this dedication from the author: «To Mr. Gustave Moreau, this "Ombre ardente," to which he was a source of such inspiration, my respectful homage and unbounded admiration.» He also expressed this admiration in his «Memoirs»: «A unique visionary, the sphere of dreams belongs to him, but he was rendered so ill by his visions that he transposed into his works his shudder of anguish and despair. He, the master sorcerer, has bewitched his era, enchanted his contemporaries and infected with idealism the end-of-the-century skepticism and practicality.» In «Mr. de Phocas» Jean Lorrain devoted an entire chapter to Moreau, describing at length the works of the man who «can boast that he has crossed over the threshold of mystery.»

The immediate predecessors of Symbolist painting were to be found in England, in the Pre-Raphaelite Brotherhood sponsored by John Ruskin, which included in its ranks Dante Gabriel Rossetti, John Everett Millais, Edward Coley Burne-Jones and William Holman Hunt. They had been known in France since 1855, when they had participated in the International Exhibition in Paris. However, there was no indication that they had much influence on French artists. They were of the same generation as Moreau, as was the Swiss Arnold Böcklin, who can also be considered a predecessor. It was approximately thirty years later that a Symbolist movement took shape, first in literature, then in painting, with exhibitions at the Café Volpini in 1889, at Le Barc de Boutteville beginning in 1891, at the Salons of the Rosicrucians, founded in 1892 under the auspices of Sâr Mérodack Joséphin Péladan, and in Brussels, with the Group of XX, from 1884 to 1893.

It was at the Café Volpini and then at Le Barc de Boutteville, that Gauguin, Emile Bernard and the Nabis, products of the School of Pont-Aven, exhibited their «synthesist» paintings. At the Salon of the Rosicrucians and in the Group of XX works were shown by Jean Toorop, Fernand Khnopff, Georges de Feure and Jean Delville (a painter and writer, the author of «Shiver of the Sphinx» and the creator of the Idealist Salon d'Art). All were Belgians or Dutchmen who, together with James Ensor, William Degouve de Nuncques and John Thorn Prikker, made, beyond the borders of France, the most important contribution to Symbolist esthetics, which were often permeated by the spirit of Art Nouveau.

In France, Maurice Denis was the main theoretician of the movement, while Charles Filiger was notable for his mysticism and his research into the geometric possibilities of art. But Odilon Redon, in spite of the undeniable Symbolist tendencies of many of his works, always remained aloof. And, according to his son Arï, he did not like to be called a Symbolist.

The same was true of Gustave Moreau. He was distrustful of all theories based on spirituality and had never yielded to Sâr Péladan's invitation to join his group. A Symbolist before there was a Symbolist movement, he never participated in their exhibitions. Moreover, both his ideas and his style distinguished him from the painters mentioned above. Edouard Schuré, in «Predecessors and Rebels,» said of him that he was «the Symbolist of the pure idea.» It is not clear just what he meant by that, but he also said, with reference to Moreau, «In every respect his art deserves the name of "psychic painting".»

It is indisputable that Moreau had a very lofty and clear idea of the spiritual values that he wanted his paintings to extol. They might take the form of a philosophical reflection on suffering or destiny, or be integrated into a mystical idealism linked with Christian thought, as we have seen in *The Life of Mankind*, which is dominated by the figure of Christ. His penchant for symbolic objects was borne out in his paintings with an abundance which was sometimes overwhelming.

As to «psychic painting,» this is a concept that can be understood in two different ways. Applied to Moreau's work, it can on the one hand refer to his tendency to try to express certain constants of human behavior through the medium of myths. But, as John Barth has written, myths «are, among other things, poetic distillations of our psychic experiences and consequently always relate to everyday reality.» On the other hand, one can interpret several aspects of Moreau's painting — the choice and repetition of themes, his favorite personages, the persistence of some ornamental elements — as being the unconscious assertion of the most obscure features of his own personality.

We have already attempted to elucidate his attitude to women. His attitude to men appears more peculiar and more difficult to define precisely. In many of his pictures there is considerable ambiguity. Such has Moreau striven to give their faces an almost feminine beauty that one might well hesitate before specifying the sex of certain personages if one did not know that their names were Apollo, Jason, Hesiod and Narcissus.

In a note about *Tyrtaeus Singing during Combat*, he stipulated that the poet «is represented as young, feminine only in the portrayal of the head, and of an antique beauty.» And, about the lyre-bearer accompanying Tyrtaeus: «This figure should have a gentle mien, be covered with draperies and very feminine. It is almost a woman.» A watercolor painted by Moreau in 1884 depicted *An Indian (Arabian) Singer* (see p. 54). In its features and also in its costume it inevitably

ITALIAN LANDSCAPE, undated. Watercolor, 3 $^{15}/_{16}$″ × 6 $^{5}/_{16}$″ (10 × 16). Gustave Moreau Museum, Paris

PORTRAIT OF ADÉLAÏDE-ALEXANDRINE DUREUX, undated.
Ink and watercolor, $6^5/_{16}'' \times 4^7/_8''$ (16 × 12.4 cm) Gustave Moreau Museum, Paris

gave the impression of being a female figure. Hence the understandable error of Emile Straus, to whom the painter had sent the watercolor, an error revealed by the fairly recent discovery at the Ephrussi de Rothschild Foundation in Saint-Jean-Cap-Ferrat, where this work is on display, of a letter by Moreau attached to the back of the *Indian Singer*:

«My dear Straus,
«I am delighted that you were pleased by my little painting. However, it is not a woman that I tried to portray. It is a young Arab boy, a poet-singer. They are said to resemble women so much that they can easily be mistaken for girls; hence your error.
«Best regards.

Gustave Moreau.»

In «Against Sainte-Beuve,» Marcel Proust, describing somewhat inaccurately the painting entitled *The Persian Poets* (Maurice Rheims Collection), spoke of the «poet with a woman's face» to evoke «a fragment of the land of Gustave Moreau.»

It is tempting — and there are those who have succumbed to this temptation — to relate this penchant for depicting feminized masculine figures to homosexual tendencies. However, nothing that is known about the painter's life can justify such a supposition, not even his friendship with his faithful and devoted Henri Rupp. Although the possibility of such an unavowed and perhaps unconscious tendency cannot be ruled out, it may well be that the portrayal of the handsome youth resulted from Moreau's pursuit of a formal idealization of the young poet and the young hero. Hero perceived their beauty as being more moving if it evoked the fragility and somewhat mysterious charm of woman. This sexual ambiguity can also be interpreted as embodying an allusion to original androgyny, an image of the primitive perfection that a pure spirit nostalgically tries to aspire to and recapture. But, as we have said, Moreau took very great care to protect the secrecy of his private life, and we should not allow ourselves to venture into the obscure territory of hypothesis.

These doubts, these shadows, these contradictions, these glimpses of impossible dreams, these fragments of indecipherable thought that take on the form of unexpected figures or unexplained symbols in Moreau's paintings, go a long way towards explaining his appeal as an artist whose works are permeated with poetic feeling. This is enough to justify the admiration bestowed on him by the Surrealists, particularly André Breton, who were more mindful of the ideological implications of a work than of its purely pictorial qualities, to which Moreau did not always give prime of place.

Having progressed from Romanticism to Symbolism via mythology, he had also discovered within himself a more mysterious taste for an art which eluded historical definition and which he summed up in these words: «The expression of human emotion, of the passion of man, undoubtedly interests me keenly; but I am less inclined to express these leanings of the mind and the spirit than, as it were, to render visible the inner flashes of lightning which we cannot connect with anything (...) and which, transmuted by the the marvelous effects of pure visual art, can open up horizons that are magical — I might even say divine.»

Gustave Moreau would perhaps have been happy to know that, eighty years after his death, as we look at his paintings, it is these «inner flashes of lightning» that hold our gaze and continue to arouse our curiosity.

JEAN SELZ

BIOGRAPHY

1826. On April 6, Gustave Moreau was born at 7, rue des Saint-Pères, Paris, the son of Louis Moreau, an architect, and Pauline Moreau, née Desmoutiers.

1827. The Moreau family settled in Vesoul.

1830. The family returned to Paris, first living at 48, rue Saint-Nicolas d'Antin, and then 16, rue des Trois-Frères (today the Rue Taitbout).

1838. Entered the Collège Rollin as a boarder, where he remained for two years.

1840. Death of his sister Camille.

1841. First trip to Italy with his mother, uncle and aunt. In Paris, he worked in the evenings in a drawing studio.

1844–46. Entered the Ecole des Beaux-Arts as a student of François Picot.

1850. Left the Ecole des Beaux-Arts. Visited Delacroix. Rented a studio at 28, avenue Frochot. Developed a close friendship with Chassériau.

1852. First submission to the Salon and first sale: *Pietà*. His father bought a townhouse at 14, rue de La Rochefoucauld.

1853. Exhibited at the Salon.

1855. Took part in the International Exhibition. The government purchased *Athenians Delivered to the Minotaur* (Museum of Bourg-en-Bresse). Exhibited in Lyons and Bordeaux.

1856. Chassériau died. *The Young Man and Death* («Tribute to Chassériau»).

1857–59. Traveled in Italy, visiting Rome, Florence, Venice, Naples, etc. Copied painters of the Renaissance. Met Edgar Degas, Elie Delaunay, Léon Bonnat, Henri Chapu and Georges Bizet.

1862. Death of his father. Painted *Stations of the Cross* for the church of Decazeville. Became a friend of Eugène Fromentin, Puvis de Chavannes and Ricard.

1864. *Œdipus and the Sphinx*, shown at the Salon, won an award.

1865. Exhibited *Jason and Medea* and *The Young Man and Death* at the Salon. Invited to the Court at Compiègne.

1866. Two paintings at the Salon: *Diomedes Devoured by his Horses* (Rouen Museum) and *Thracien Girl Carrying Orpheus's Head* (Louvre).

1867. Took part in the International Exhibition.

1869. Won an award at the Salon, where he showed *Prometheus, Jupiter and Europa* and two watercolors.

1875. Made Chevalier de la Légion d'honneur.

1876. At the Salon: *Hercules and the Lernaean Hydra, Salomé Dancing before Herod* and *The Apparition*.

1878. Six oils and five watercolors shown at the International Exhibition.

1880. Last submission to the Salon: *Galatea* and *Helen on the Walls of Troy*.

1882. Exhibited twenty-five watercolors illustrating the «Fables» of La Fontaine at the Cercle des Aquarellistes in the Rue Lafitte.

1883. Made an officer of the Légion d'honneur.

1884. Started *The Chimeras. The Life of Mankind*. His mother died.

1885. (?) Trip to the Netherlands and Belgium.

1886. Exhibited sixty-four watercolors illustrating the «Fables» of La Fontaine at the Goupil Gallery.

1888. Elected a member of the Académie des Beaux-Arts.

1889. Took part in the International Exhibition.

1890. Death of his friend Adélaïde-Alexandrine Dureux.

1891. Appointed teacher at the Ecole des Beaux-Arts.

1894. Commissioned by the State to do a sketch for a Gobelin tapestry: *The Poet and the Siren*.

1896. *Jupiter and Sémélé*.

1897. Sketches for *Dead Lyres*.

1898. Moreau died on April 18, bequeathing to the State his house in the Rue de La Rochefoucauld, together with all the works in it.

1903. Opening of the Gustave Moreau Museum, with Georges Rouault as its first curator.

EXHIBITIONS

1886. Watercolors. Goupil Gallery, Paris.

1906. 209 works. Georges Petit Gallery, Paris. Preface to catalogue by Robert de Montesquiou.

1926. Gustave Moreau and some of his pupils, Paris.

1961. 145 works. Louvre. Preface to catalogue by Jean Cassou and Jean Paladhile.

1962. Gustave Moreau and his pupils. Cantini Museum, Marseilles.

1964. Baden-Baden and Neuss, West Germany.

1965. National Museum of Western Art, Tokyo.

1966. Trieste, Italy.

1974. Gustave Moreau and his pupils. Beaux-Arts Museum, Bordeaux. Yokohama, Hiroshima and Tokyo. Preface to catalogue by Jean Chapelain, René Huyghe and Gilberte Martin-Méry. Gustave Moreau. Los Angeles County Museum of Arts. Preface to catalogue by Julius Kaplan.

BIBLIOGRAPHY

1900. ARY RENAN: *Gustave Moreau*. Paris.

1901. GUSTAVE LARROUMET: *Notice historique sur la vie et les œuvres de M. Gustave Moreau*. Paris.

1912. *L'Œuvre de Gustave Moreau*. Introduction by Georges Desvallières. Paris.

1913. LÉON DESHAIRS and JEAN LARAN: *Gustave Moreau*. Paris.

1914. HENRY ROUJON ed.: *Gustave Moreau*. Paris.

1960. RAGNAR VON HOLTEN: *L'Art fantastique de Gustave Moreau*. Paris.

1971. JEAN PALADHILE, JOSÉ PIERRE: *Gustave Moreau*. Paris.

1972. BARBARA WRIGHT and PIERRE NOISY: *Gustave Moreau et Eugène Fromentin*. Hitherto unpublished correspondence. La Rochelle.

1974. JULIUS KAPLAN: *Gustave Moreau*. Los Angeles.

1976. PIERRE-LOUIS MATHIEU: *Gustave Moreau. With a catalogue of the finished paintings, watercolors and drawings*. Boston, Mass.

★

Film. *Gustave Moreau*. 35 mm. Producer: Nelly Kaplan. Commentators: Nelly Kaplan, A. Breton, L. Bellon, J. Martin, J. Squinquel. Music: J. Ledrut. Photography: F. Bogard. Office de la documentation par le Film, Paris, 1961.

We wish to thank the owners of the pictures by Gustave Moreau reproduced in this book:

MUSEUMS

CANADA

National Gallery, Ottawa.

FRANCE

Gustave Moreau, Paris – Louvre Museum, Paris – Museum of the Petit-Palais, Paris – Musée des Beaux-Arts, Rouen.

GERMANY

Städelsches Kunstinstitut und Städtische Galerie, Frankfurt – Clemens Sels Museum, Neuss.

UNITED KINGDOM.

Museum and Art Gallery, Bristol – National Gallery, London – Victoria and Albert Museum, London.

U.S.A.

Art Institute, Chicago – Wadsworth Atheneum, Hartford, Conn. – Metropolitan Museum of Art, New York – Fogg Art Museum, Harvard University, Cambridge, Mass.

PRIVATE COLLECTIONS

The Armand Hammer Foundation, Los Angeles – The Ephrussi de Rothshild Foundation, St. Jean-Cap-Ferrat – and the collectors who did not wish to be mentioned.

ILLUSTRATIONS